I0605224

CYRUS CASSELLS

EVERYTHING IN LIFE IS RESURRECTION

Books by Cyrus Cassells

Poetry
The Mud Actor (1982)
Soul Make a Path through Shouting (1994)
Beautiful Signor (1997)
More Than Peace and Cypresses (2004)
The Crossed-Out Swastika (2012)
The Gospel according to Wild Indigo (2018)
More Than Watchmen at Daybreak (2020)
The World That the Shooter Left Us (2022)
Is There Room for Another Horse on Your Horse Ranch? (2024)
Everything in Life is Resurrection: Selected Poems, 1982-2022 (2025)
Lorca to the Umpteenth Power (2026)

Translations
Still Life with Children: Selected Poems of Francesc Parcerisas (2019)
To the Cypress Again and Again: Tribute to Salvador Espriu (2023)

Nonfiction
Blackbird: How Black Musicians Sang the Beatles into Being—and Sang Back to Them Ever After (2023)

CYRUS CASSELLS
EVERYTHING IN LIFE IS RESURRECTION:
SELECTED POEMS, 1982–2022

WITH AN INTRODUCTION BY ELLEN HINSEY

TCU PRESS
FORT WORTH, TEXAS

TCU TEXAS POET LAUREATE SERIES

Library of Congress Cataloging-in-Publication Data

Names: Cassells, Cyrus, author. | Hinsey, Ellen, 1960- writer of introduction.
Title: Everything in life is resurrection : selected poems, 1982-2022 / Cyrus Cassells ; with an introduction by Ellen Hinsey.
Description: Fort Worth, Texas : TCU Press, 2025. | Series: TCU Texas poet laureate series | Includes bibliographical references. | Summary: "Drawn from eight acclaimed books of poetry and spanning forty years, Everything in Life is Resurrection: Selected Poems, 1982-2022, is 2021 Texas Poet Laureate Cyrus Cassells's long-awaited retrospective volume. Ellen Hinsey, in her compelling introduction, 'A Lyric Poet in Dark Times,' heralds Cassells as 'America's foremost lyric poet, who, under the pressure of adverse circumstances, has turned from his home in music to unflinchingly face the blood and havoc of his era's civil sphere.' In addition, Hinsey lauds Cassells's always riveting language 'characterized throughout by a highly visual and expressive vocabulary, one touched by the grandeur of Shakespeare and the authority of the King James Bible.' Mark Doty has said: 'The astonishing lyric fabric of Cassells's work is weighted, as true lyrics of the earth must be, with the sorrow and cruelty of history... one side of the song doesn't cancel out the other; they are held, in Cassells's sweeping oratorios, side by side.'"-- Provided by publisher.
Identifiers: LCCN 2024046905 | ISBN 9780875659091 (cloth)
Subjects: LCGFT: Poetry.
Classification: LCC PS3553.A7955 E94 2025 | DDC 811/.54--dc23/eng/20241011
LC record available at https://lccn.loc.gov/2024046905

TCU Press
TCU BOX 298300
Fort Worth, TX 76129
www.tcupress.com

Designed by Adrienne Martinez

THIS BOOK IS IN MEMORY OF MY MOTHER
MARY ISABEL WILLISTON CASSELLS
(1935–2006)

19

CONTENTS

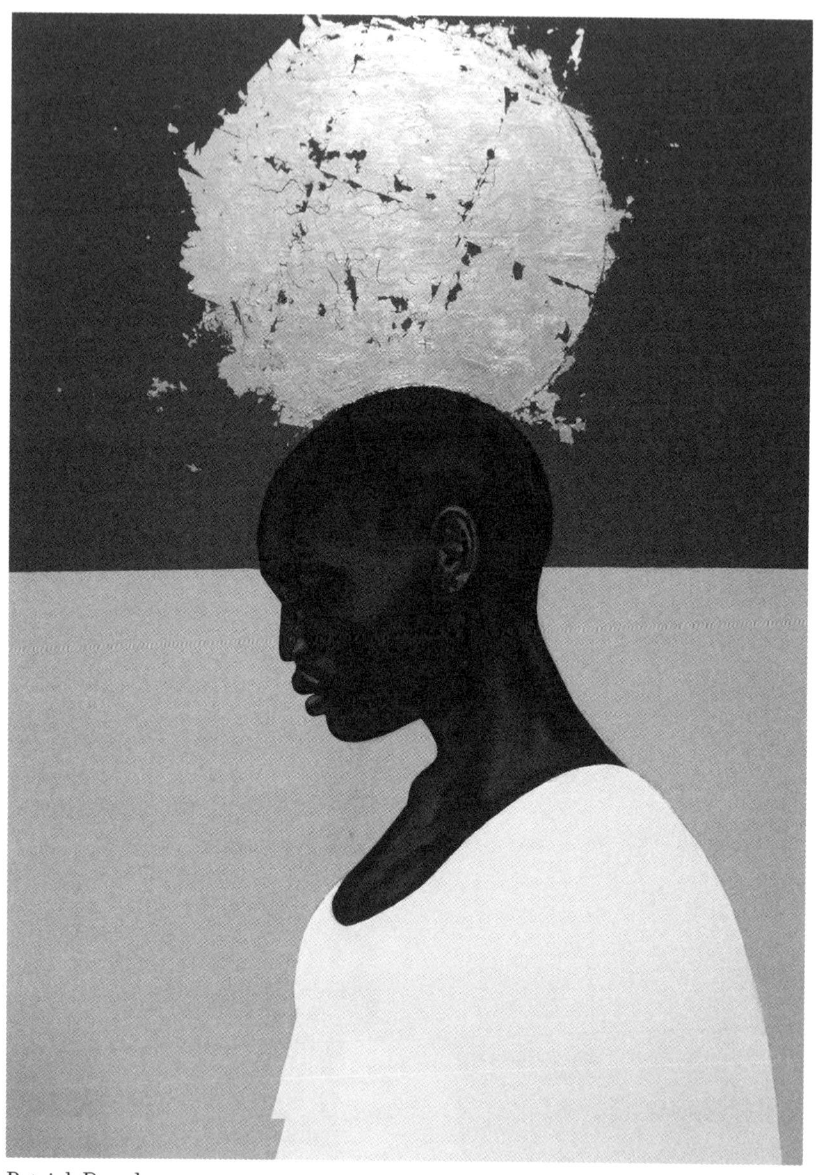

Patrick Dougher
GOD ABOVE II (2018)
Acrylic/ Gold Leaf on Canvas - 30" x 40"

INTRODUCTION

Cyrus Cassells, A Lyric Poet in Dark Times

Ellen Hinsey

I.

No poet can choose the time into which they are born. This simple fact is responsible for the complexity but also the richness of the poetic tradition. It can sometimes happen that a poet is intrinsically suited to their time—Petrarch's sonnets have come to characterize an entire era. In those moments, so propitious to the music of poetry, we witness the emergence of some of the art's most sublime achievements. But in reality few poets live a life free from historical "hinge" moments—abrupt political, social, or religious upheavals in which strife, suffering, disharmony, discrimination, and blood emerge as dominant features. Such is the case with the poetic lifework of Cyrus Cassells, America's foremost lyric poet, who, under the pressure of adverse circumstances, has turned from his home in music to unflinchingly face the blood and destruction of his era's civil sphere.

While the idea may seem increasingly anachronistic, it is a given that for lyric poets, such as Rilke, poetry is an art that is not chosen, but bestowed—taking root in their hearing and manifesting in dimensions beyond their will. This is certainly true of Cassells, whose work was first characterized by a lyricism that burrowed deep into its texture. In his second, much acclaimed volume *Soul Make a Path Through Shouting,* we find the following lines:

> The first lightning-white rose dying to open
> Beneath the systole and diastole of a starry night,
> Bee-yellows, butter-yellows, sweet-simmering-hay-yellows,
> Iris, allium, the proffered chalices of tulips
> (The colors of a fabulous dusk in Tunisia).
>
> ("Down from the Houses of Magic")

Here, Cassells is already in complete command of his technique, something that expands throughout the eight collections represented in this retrospective volume. His language, characterized throughout by a highly visual and expressive vocabulary, is touched by the grandeur of Shakespeare and the authority of the King James Bible. There is a love of verb and noun, a richness of consonance and assonance, and a voluptuousness that makes a feast of description. As readers, we are generously invited to the table, as when the poet awakens in Italy:

> Sunday: the market's still, the street,
> gossipless and serene.
> Above the basilica,
> the Roman sky blooms,
> as never before,
> and I must wake you,
> give you this view,
> garnet, roseate, gill-blue–
> A gull delights
> in San Giovanni's façade,
> the pale row of mystics,
> passing from crown to crown–
>
> ("Love Poem of the Roman Days,"*Beautiful Signor*)

In this, Cassells aligns with the great traditions of love and erotic lyrics, affirming that, despite life's difficult passages, sexuality is an integral part of our shared human journey. He writes about the love between men with an unmatched beauty, complexity, and restraint that is reminiscent of classical literature:

> And I find in you
> the ochre and gold,
> the lustrous, silvery green
> of the olive fields above Assisi.
> And I find in you
> the ineffable pink
> of the renowned saint's
> open palms,
> the white, like fountain foam,
> of an unabashed
> almond in bloom,
> find in you
> the sky with a linnet-blue
> of our Brother Wind's scapular (...)

("The Risk-Takers," *Beautiful Signor*)

In such poems of exaltation and celebration, love encounters occur amid life's unfolding mystery, and sexuality is reduced to neither politics nor sensation, but is something infinitely more complex, while never lessening its carnal power. Had Cassells had the chance to live his life in a historical moment of grace, this might have been the legacy he bequeathed to us, and we would not have been the poorer for this gift.

But, as we know, this has not been the case. For in fact, even in Cassells's first volumes, the poems already pointed to a second, and equally important theme, that of the darknesses of the world. At such times we recall Auden's famous lines dedicated to W. B. Yeats: "Mad Ireland hurt you into poetry." Similarly, into the life of this most gifted lyric poet have come the traumatic generational events and unending violence of our chaotic, politically polarized and destructive world—events that, as in Yeats's lifetime, change both the poet and his poetry. If Yeats's early poetry was characterized by the perfect music of a poem such as *The Song of Wandering Aengus*, we know that Ireland's civil war, which Yeats experienced at the height of his powers, would force Ireland's pre-eminent lyric poet to bear witness to the life- and art-altering violence that appeared at his door:

We are closed in, and the key is turned
On our uncertainty; somewhere
A man is killed, or a house burned.
Yet no clear fact to be discerned:
Come build in the empty house of the stare.

Indeed, in his first National Poetry Series Award–winning volume *The Mud Actor* and the subsequent *Soul Make a Path Through Shouting*, Cassells had in fact already foretold, in the early plague years of AIDS, some of the trials to come:

Anoint me
When I say outright:
In the plague time, my heart
Was tested,
My living soul
Struck like a tower bell,
Once, twice,
Four times in a single season.

In *Soul Make a Path through Shouting*, the "testing of the heart" also encompasses the blinding injustices that will lead to the civil rights movement—the subject of the eponymous poem—as well as elegies to victims of Nazi violence, including the heart-rending *Poem for the Artists of the Holocaust,* included in this volume. This is a subject Cassells will return to in his fifth volume *The Crossed-Out Swastika (2012),* which confronts the history and extreme violence of the twentieth century. In this collection Cassells's language is honed to a fine edge; it has become stripped down as it faces the unlanguagable, as in his poem "The Ravine," which addresses the "Holocaust by Bullets" in Ukraine:

THE RAVINE

In my fifth
holy year on earth,

undeterred,
I climbed out of a corpse-filled,

breaksprit ravine,
clutching the roots of trees

(so beautiful,
the god-tall cypresses,

the grandfather pines
in that part of the Crimea),

and groped my way, gingerly,
toward my twilit village,

the lone, itinerant survivor.
The pull, the rose light

of home
is unkillable.

At such moments, as readers, we follow Cassells as he makes his way forward with a single lamp in his attempt to light the darkness. Alerting us as well that such darknesses are always edged by new and ever-advancing darknesses.

II.

Cyrus Cassells has spoken about the "permeability" of the poet's house—or as the Nobel Prize–winning poet Czesław Miłosz so aptly put it, "our house is open, there are no keys in the doors /and invisible guests come in and out at will." As is clear throughout Cassells's work, the role of the poet as witness is not only a chosen responsibility, but also something intrinsic to the poetic act. The poet hears their time. As with the work of the major American poets Ai, Audre Lorde, and Adrienne Rich, who—along with the European poets Federico García Lorca, Constantine Cavafy, Pier Paolo Pasolini, and Cesare Pavese—are part of Cassells's poetic lineage, when we read the poet's work over the last four decades, we are aware that the music he hears is intrinsically intertwined with the noise of the world's destruction:

> His renegade instrument
>
> mangled
> Under the haggard weight
>
> of winter-killed, unraveling men.
> Music at the brink of the grave (…)
>
> ("Juliek's Violin," *The Crossed-Out Swastika*)

In Cassells's eighth book, *The World That the Shooter Left Us*, the poet unflinchingly addresses the countless deaths of Black Americans, victims of police and racist violence with its illogic and soul-testing grief. Alongside America's endemic racism, Cassells has endured the aftermath of so-called "personal tragedies," including the shooting of an associate's parent in "common crossfire," as well as the impact of the murders of Michael Brown, Eric Garner, and George Floyd—well-known names that represent a fraction of the deaths due to what Cassells has labeled "the theater of excessive force" that continues unabated.

At the start of our new century, the German poet Ingeborg Bachman's prophesy has disturbingly come to pass: "War is no longer declared, only continued. The monstrous has become everyday." The present volume of selected poems opens with the eponymous poem *The World That the Shooter Left Us* and speaks to these dangers ever-present on home ground:

THE WORLD THAT THE SHOOTER LEFT US

In this one, ladies and gentlemen,
Beware, be clear: the brown man,

The able lawyer, the paterfamilias,
Never makes it out of the poem alive:

The rash, all-too-daily report,
The out-of-the-blue bullet

Blithely shatters our treasured
Legal eagle's bones and flesh—

In the brusque spectacle of point-blank force,
On a crimsoned street,

Where a revered immigrant plummets
Over a contested parking spot,

And the far-seeing sages insist,
Amid strident maenads

Of at-the-ready patrol car sirens,
Clockwork salvos,

The charismatic Latino lawyer's soul
Is banished, elsewhere, without a shred

Of eloquence in the matter—

The World That the Shooter Left Us hurts us into facing what must be clearly stated— as the only way to make a path towards justice:

A Taser is not an answer
A rushing bullet is not a dream

There is no sunny god
In an Apollo Helmet

A livelong mercenary is not
A frisking meadow lamb

Lady Justice is no
Fearsome chimera

No lurking drone
No business-as-usual Cerberus

A callous Caesar is not
A far-seeing Christ—

"Is Not" (Don't Interrupt the Sorrow)

With *The World That the Shooter Left Us* Cassells comes full circle, returning to a promise made in *Soul Make a Path through Shouting:*

Still craving a robust
Tenderness and justice,
I will go on living
With all I have seen.

It is little wonder that Cassells has been the recipient of many awards for both his teaching and poetry, including the Peter I. B. Lavan Poets Award, the Poetry Society's William Carlos Williams Award, a Lambda Literary Award, as well as fellowships from the Guggenheim Foundation, the Lannan Foundation, and the National Endowment for the Arts, to name but a few. A major poet, the importance of his work has only continued to grow over the decades. Most importantly, Cassells's poetry is touched by grace and at the center is a stalwart belief in the Other. It is highly symbolic that this long-overdue volume of selected poems should be entitled *Everything in Life is Resurrection*. Cassells is, and will continue to be, a carrier of the blessed light that—despite the world's "negation and despair"—continues to show "an affirming flame."

Paris, May 2024

from
The World That the Shooter Left Us (2022)

THE WORLD THAT THE SHOOTER LEFT US

(Stand Your Ground)

In this one, ladies and gentlemen,
Beware, be clear: the brown man,

The able lawyer, the paterfamilias,
Never makes it out of the poem alive:

The rash, all-too-daily report,
The out-of-the-blue bullet

Blithely shatters our treasured
Legal eagle's bones and flesh—

In the brusque spectacle of point-blank force,
On a crimsoned street,

Where a revered immigrant plummets
Over a contested parking spot,

And the far-seeing sages insist,
Amid strident maenads

Of at-the-ready patrol car sirens,
Clockwork salvos,

The charismatic Latino lawyer's soul
Is banished, elsewhere, without a shred

Of eloquence in the matter—
And the brute, churning

Surfaces of the world,

They bear our beloved citizen away—

Which means, austere saints
And all-seeing masters,

If I grasp your bracing challenge:
At our lives' most brackish hour,

Our highest mission isn't just to bawl,
But to turn the soul-shaking planet

Of the desecrated parking lot
(The anti-miracle),

The blunt, vitriolic white man's
Unnecessary weapon,

And the ruse of self-defense
Into justice-cries and ballots?

Into newfound pledges,
And particles of light?

in memory of J. Garza, 1949-2017

IS NOT (DON'T INTERRUPT THE SORROW)

A Taser is not an answer
A rushing bullet is not a dream

There is no sunny god
In an Apollo Helmet

A livelong mercenary is not
A frisking meadow lamb

Lady Justice is no
Fearsome chimera

No lurking drone
No business-as-usual Cerberus

A callous Caesar is not
A far-seeing Christ—

*

Listen: a blazing Mississippi cross
Never presages a messiah.

A daffodil in a "sundown town" never signals
The onset of spring—

*

So after two callous seasons,
I finally dared to inquire

If his taken-too-soon father's ousting
"Stand Your Ground" assassin

Was indeed white, "lily-white"
& naturally his response

In this volatile demesne,
This gallery of averted eyes

& gimcrack defenders galore
Was yes

Dear God of course yes

*

Don't interrupt the sorrow
A woman croons

But all I catch is the *ack-ack-ack*
Of ink-blotter redaction,

The X-rated sputter of a black site's
Water-boarded man

Or a flailing cigarette seller,
Cuffed, gasping for air,

Jinxing arm & insignia
Marring his throat:

Is not

Is not

Is not

Is not—

in memory of Eric Garner, 1970-2014

FINDING AMERICA IN GOYA'S "BLACK PAINTINGS"

Today, in the Prado's lower gallery, I perceive
Our ailing country's fast-galloping infamy

In Goya's unflinching "Black Paintings."
Our vaunted democracy floundering

Like the Iberian master's sweet, beseeching
Mutt in a panic,

As Sir Insolvent Mountebank
Runs extravagantly amok—

And how many swastikas and hailstones?
How many catcalls and rapes per hour?—

Through the misted country's spectral atmosphere,
Like Francisco's sooty, scourging colossus—

Meanwhile, in a sorcerer's nocturnal spell,
Señoritas Veracity and Sanity,

Those slandered and jettisoned sisters,
Slowly and fearfully lift, in jeopardy,

From accursed terra firma—hapless
Victims of the genius court painter's

Blood-soaked trio of wing-hatted warlocks
Levitating in a feral frenzy—

THE HOOD

(Abu Ghraib & Vietnam)

O desert corporal,
You of the cardboard pedestal

& scandalous wires,
The dungeon's ink-dark cloth,

Nobody in the instilling army has a clue
You're the very same child

Who stumbled & fumbled to reach
A dilapidated shed,

Failed to fit your first grade limbs
Into a dingy crawlspace:

All of six—how could you shadow-box
Pterodactyl jungle choppers, grasp

Phantoms of round-eyed
Bar girls in ripped *ao dai?*

You raise a rum-flecked pillow
To ward off the predictable blows

From your dashing,
Dish-breaking,

Back from country Dad,
And damned if he doesn't

Scissor the homespun pillowcase
Just to dub you a new Casper—

Little huffing captive
In a funereal cowl,

A lowly chador—
To consign his bullish firstborn,

His little boy hellion,
Back to a claiming darkness:

Here comes the hood in childhood!

CLARINET

At my family's stained window,
A morning jay.

I stop my scissoring,
As if I could reclaim

A Santiago of bird-call
And sudden ease,

As if I could annul
The battle-gray maze of gutting

Jails, courthouses, morgues—
Purgatory where I bend

Over the burlap,
Again and again,

To show the blunt,
Still disillusioning world

The smashed black bell
Of your clarinet.

A blue swatch of your work-shirt becomes
The irrevocable, raw dusk

Of that day;
Here, in this farrago of scraps,

Your living room as I found it:
Lunatic with ripped song sheets...

In imploring red,
A beggar's scuffed vermilion,

I've stitched:
Whoever sees my arpillera,

Help me to pray for my son.
He was seen leaving rehearsal

At 7 o'clock.
He was seen in detention

At Londres #38.
He was seen; he was seen...

After so many years, perhaps
You wouldn't recognize me, Leonel;

I've become the weatherworn,
Undocile woman

Manacled to a tyrant's fence,
A mother dancing the *gueca* solo

In the monitored plaza,
The ache of my make-do arms

Trumpeted,
Your rakish college photo

Pinned to my wind-riffled blouse:
In the *arpillera*,

A tiny, vivid, appliquéd doll,
Forever mourning,

Forever swaying
To your unforgettable woodwind.

ICEBOX

II. THOSE "RETURN TO SENDERS" CHILDREN

Separated, the borrowing, the castaway children were blessed with standard American scraps or Chiclets stale cookies wrapped little sweets or hectored, quiet as it's kept, to caress the penises and vulvas of strangers or for their own to be inspected: *Can you keep a secret, Miguel, Maria?* Despite their demerits head lice recalcitrant smell, the border-despising, fundamentally invasive minors were allotted, each to each, their quintessential moment in court, courtesy of almighty Justice, as meted by the greatest country and economy on earth, by the ablest president on the planet. The filth-caked children were, by His gospel and righteous directive, despised sprayed with a winnowing hose at the sacrosanct border slapped seized tear gassed caged shunted to ex-internment camps holding pens sally ports forbidden to hug herded under fusty bridges handed with machine-swift severity & clarity to professionals ogres sleepwalkers ill-equipped teens gangs gruff border police ambitious privateers yes even wily traffickers lust-filled clients maybe over a thousand illegal children—oops!—like so many stamped but still dust-strewn packages the careworn postman mislaid during the bustling Christmas season: *Look, here's a tasty servant-girl-in-training, a surefire ten! Here's a little cherub—a pouty, long-lashed boy, perfect for a secret movie…*

III. ICEBOX

The place where the ensnared children are held
Is sometimes dubbed an "icebox,"

Because of ICE custody, clearly,
But also because

Gelid air is piped, without cease,
Into their fetid cages,

Which must make the baffled kids
Equivalent to frozen peas or chicken;

Yes, chicken is exactly
What some of the boys will become—

COURAGE SONG FOR SCOTT WARREN

Sing: no more makeshift crosses
In the gangplank desert,

No more "dogcatcher trucks,"
No more jawbones under the moon—

Bring your rebellious grit,
Like a bromide or a borderland candle,

To our bigotry-is-commonplace republic's
Chaos. Bold anima, dissenting angel,

Among the betraying cliffs and dry washes,
The yellow plumes of the *palo verde,*

Be runagate Harriet in a midnight cane field
(General Tubman!), be Martin bravely writing

In an abysmal Birmingham jail.
Yes, your boundless shepherd's gallantry,

Your on-tap compassion
Is the rescuing sip

And the heaven-sent gourd required
At all our desperate crossings.

from

More Than Watchmen at Daybreak (2020)

I. WINTER ABBEY WITH VENUS RISING

Pilgrim, under in-a-rush chevrons
Of restless desert clouds,

At shape-shifting winter's onset,
Picture the Benedictines' elating valley,

Its eminent gusts yielding
A Yuletide jackpot of curt,

Valedictory leaves—whirling, marshaling
In windswept cardinal directions:

Broadcast realm of *glory be*, insurgent
Kingdom of *kyrie eleison*—

Solstice: a slowly ascending,
Bold as a horseman sun

Burnishes each antediluvian cliff,
Each telltale winter crest,

With its equalizing gaze:
A resolute, dispassionate topaz—

Far from the deriding republic,
A mint-new Herod's decrees,

The poignant bronze of reed beds,
The strict rhythm of the liturgical hours,

And later, as irrepressible Venus rises,
Consecrating the far-flung abbey,

And the stalwart compass star appears,
The ink of darkened, sacramental banks

With pallid embroideries of ice,
The blessed Jerusalem of the pewter river—

VII. MARY'S DAY

Wait! This hour of circling kestrels
And callous sentries' dice,

This rain-undoing Friday
Of unremitting nails—

Clarified by mordant daylight
And searing torchlight,

Hear me out,
Is also Mary's day:

Mary the mourner,
The peerless maker, the harrowed

Witness to her son's
Desecrated body, human majesty

That can never be recovered,
Not by hyssop or unceasing prayer—

Mary the fearless, intent listener,
Forever bending to gauge

The tenor of her small son's cough—

X. CELESTIAL PRAYERS

As Christ in his desert crucible
Became brother to the limitless, starry sky,

There's never a lucent night
In the outlying hermitage

When I'm not a loyal son
Or a half-besotted cousin

To all-centering Polaris,
Watch-me-everyone Sirius, and The Northern Cross—

Listen, on my tenth birthday, I was taught,
By my assiduous pilot father,

The sundial's impetus,
The red-hot equator's pivotal role,

And the passkey beauty
Of springtime constellations—

In the cricket-praised valley,
Where witching hour or wolf's hour

Clarity is the reigning king,
Sometimes I dream

Of opening my mendicant mouth
(Delicate as a gilded carp's

Or a leaping dolphin's rictus),
And letting the unfailing night

Feed me its impossible provender
Of planets and prodigal stars,

Or keener, better, richer:
Bless me with celestial prayers.

XII. MORE THAN WATCHMEN AT DAYBREAK

The river's soft pistons, the river's black silk
Under shooting stars—

The voluble ink and silver-white sky
Looming above the stark monastery

Becomes the coppice elk's vast eternity—
The duenna moon,

All at once coquettish,
Brash as sin, blanches

The river-curve, the heron,
The corral of fast-asleep horses—

August: the souls says,
Yes, I was there:

When raffish, runaway flames
Claimed the orphanage,

When rampant smoke drove the dying
Into the summer sea;

Present when riled protestors cried
If they fire into the crowd...

And then they fired into the crowd;
When the aghast stranger, fingering

A galling dungeon photo, asked,
What kind of God would allow *that*?—

More than fleet, querying owls,
More than nightlong watchmen,

Born wide-awake and dying, I confess
Not even this wondrous colossus

Of shooting stars,
The extravagant earth's countless beauties

Seem capable of quenching this lust,
This innermost hunger for return—

Incensed and restive
In this desert monastery,

Thirsty, fallible, but not yet resigned,
Full of questions and parrying,

Lord Buddha, God of Abraham.
From wolf's hour to blue hour

To burgeoning dawn—

from

The Gospel According to Wild Indigo (2018)

From THE GOSPEL ACCORDING TO WILD INDIGO

The pine-tree sweetens my body.
The white iris beautifies me.

—Wallace Stevens, "In the Carolinas"

I. DAYCLEAN

Dayclean's the Gullah word
for the gala sun, the looked-for

melon, meticulous,
up-and-coming,

impossibly hale,
ecstatically gilding

the Canaan of marshlands,
lowcountry cosmos of scurrying

punchclock crabs,
dauntless kingfishers, frolicking

estuary herons—
Dayclean caresses

the praise houses—
eoho, eoho—

A's boy-time tree house
nestled in a Galahad

ancient oak.
Gold takes the street musician's

dented coronet—
Why's he still up?

Why's he still playing?—
burnishes the early-bird fingers

on a Mount Pleasant porch,
tea-brown Merlin fingers

fashioning palmetto roses,
palmetto crosses—

Crab castle, Jew's harp,
foxglove, sea junk,

marsh bridge, stilt house,
the white of hominy

and fine-sifted flour;
Lady's Island, Cat Island,

Daufuskie, St. Helena...
Rummaging gold matter-of-factly

gleans them all—
shell colors and dories,

rugged shrimp-sellers
and wind-blessed reeds—

rapacious gold.
Dayclean, dayclean:

sun like a schoolgirl
eager for show-and-tell.

VIII. CAESARS AND DREAMERS

The pharaohs of rice and indigo, the conniving
Caesars of cotton,

what were we to them?
Profitable: able

bodies from Barbados
and the Windward Coast,

the Rice Coast,
our souls ramshackle,

less than a rooster's
or a rock's.

And yet, in painstaking fields,
in joyous praise houses,

our tenacious "Go Down, Moses,"
our stirring, rallying

"In the beauty of the lilies
Christ was born across the sea..."

might have served as proof
to those zealous Southern despots

that we possessed
some quilt scrap of God.

Go tell those greed-swayed
kings of sugar, those implacable

princes of tobacco,
how we garnered freedom

in our hardscrabble dreams,
sang it as sweat-drenched,

unshakable hallelujah,
whispered it as healing salve

to allay the defiling
stripes on our backs.

Unstinting overseer,
iron-eyed Caesar,

who better to define freedom
than a slave?

IX. WILD INDIGO, BECAUSE

When rice was our nemesis
and callous-making cotton,

and the onus
of a Satan-hot tobacco

seemed to stain
our very souls,

beyond the spirit-choking
pesthouses of Sullivan Island

(our Ellis Island),
beyond the dust and ragtag

squalor of slave row,
we found a dew-soaked,

purplish blue
in the needed time—

imagine,
in a siren patch

behind the blacksmith's—
a God-sent and doe-wild blue.

X. THE WHITE IRIS BEAUTIFIES ME

Not the white of hard-won cotton,
or of pitiless snow—

I've found a whiteness
that gives me its glory;

it blooms
in Master Bellemare's garden,

and though it is, by all accounts,
untouchable,

quiet as it's kept, I've carried it
into the shabbiest of cabins,

worn it as I witnessed
the slave-breaker,

the hanging tree;
in dream-snatches

it blesses me, and I become
more than a brand,

a pretty chess piece:
at the mistress' bell,

always prudent and afraid,
wily and afraid—

And when the day comes,
my rescuing flower's name

will become my daughter's;
a freeborn woman,

I swear,
she will never be shoeless

in January snow.
Bold Iris,

she will never fear sale
or the bottom of the sea.

XVIII. THE GOSPEL ACCORDING TO WILD INDIGO

In time, the sea-loved Carolinas,
the spade-and-hoe land

which was our break-soul
yoke and lament,

became, so help us, our land.
On Lady's Island, Cat Island,

Daufuskie, St. Helena,
Ham's un-lauded children,

broken and unbroken, we waded
in the mothering water,

garnering the Moses-wise
marshes' secrets,

the irrepressible crabs' broadcasts.
Under-the-Dipper dreamers, singers,

we let ancient oaks counsel us,
mossy Abrahams and Isaacs.

From pliant sweetgrass we coaxed
mint-new forms

of utility and beauty.
We learned resilience—

who better to define freedom
than a slave?—

a taproot waiting,
from the gospel according to wild indigo,

in which death and defiling
bondage are transformed

into foam and fish-scale blue,
a heron's swoop,

and bold-fisted hurricanes dismantle
the masters' belligerence—

Our prophet-smashing owners,
our slyly disowning fathers,

they told us we had no rights
to the dawn,

and gave us first instead
the gorgon's heart of the hold,

thick as blackstrap syrup.
But here it comes—

can we get a witness?
Here it comes,

with a runagate's swiftness—
eoho, eoho!—

night-yoked mother,
never-defeated brother, sister:

inspiriting,
down-to-the-wire,

immaculate
as a deacon's gloves:

dayclean.

JASMINE

These are the days of jasmine in Rome—
when headlong, emboldened April has dissolved,

and the joyous braiding of sun and rain
brings this sweet, steady broadcast;

when I step from the suppertime train,
that's what greets me:

Roman hedges and walkways,
graffiti-laden precincts graced

with pallid fireworks, so even
the most tumbledown niches seem

breeze-swept,
festive now with fragrance—

Jasmine—the elating moment's shibboleth,
the cool, enrapturing night's cavalry—

Even crone-glorious Daria,
my terrace-loving neighbor, confides:

When Galliano came back from the front,
his right hand was bandaged,

but in his uninjured one,
ah, poet, he held

a fistful of jasmine he'd picked
along the path to my door.

How could I not become his wife?

LAZARETTO

In Trieste one sultry July I stayed
on "Old Lazaretto,"

a long port street that the adroit poet
Umberto Saba revered.

Lazaretto, the locals informed me,
means the behemoth

of a brick hospital,
shipshape for the moribund,

as well as a severe, quarantined boat,
a gray-souled station

for foundering seafarers—
Ambling the adjacent harbor, I faced

an open stretch of sea,
tranquil, stately beyond belief,

a blue, allaying mirror,
but I never encountered

a guide willing to impart
the origins of the old lazaretto,

a soul able to usher me
to the actual site, where Death prevailed,

tireless as a forest partisan—

*

At final count, eleven funeral parlors
refused his beloved's body,

so harried Raphael was charged
to hurry it into earth on his own;

granted, that was at the onset
of the winnowing AIDS years—

remember?—
when no physician could discern

the source of the ambushing disease.
It wasn't just disgust, all-out disavowal

that made the wary shunt
the stricken men with garish lesions:

fear is the quickest contagion—

*

Lazar house, pesthouse,
and in its most musical form, lazaretto—

Listen, in those lazaretto years
of fraught cell counts, mounting pills,

and spiraling hospices, rife
with featureless walls, I recall:

the tame and mannerly
failed us, yes, timidity and etiquette,

that Romulus and Remus,
were wholly decimated,

so that we were cast adrift, bereft
of any steadying map

or outright destination,
though, to be solicitous,

we were inclined to ask:
What are you feeling?

How are you today?
Then the answer might come

from a downcast "disco Apollo,"
or even your dearest friend,

a dancer/choreographer barely thirty,
reliant suddenly on an ominous cane

because his once expressive legs
were collapsing—

*

Hear me, when myriad, no longer hale
men left us,

and my bustling "City by the Bay,"
the city that thrilled us,

became a lazaretto,
I was a first-time lover,

a questing seeker
in the first months of outbreak,

of mystery and runaway mourning—
I speak for the shattered,

the aggrieved but still-alive,
the voluminous missing,

when I say once more:
Fear is the quickest contagion—

I can't believe I survived.

ELEGY WITH A GOLD CRADLE

Now that you're forever
ministering wind and turquoise, ashes

eclipsed by the sea's thrust
and the farthest tor

(I know you were always
more than my mother)—

giveaway flecks tipped and scattered
from an island palisade—

Now that you're a restless synonym
for the whistling fisherman's

surfacing mesh,
the alluring moon's path and progress

through a vast chaos
of unrelenting waves,

let me reveal:
in the at-a-loss days

following your scattering,
in my panoramic hotel, I found

a sun-flooded cradle—
so pristine, so spotlit and sacramental

beside my harbor-facing bed,
I couldn't bear to rock

or even touch it, Mother:
I marveled at the gold-leafed bars

and contours—the indomitable,
antique wood beneath, an emblem

of unbeatable hope
and prevailing tenderness—

then, for a crest-like, hallowing hour,
listen, my mourning was suffused

with the specter of your lake-calm
cascade of hair, inkwell-dark

in the accruing shadows,
your rescuing, soothing contralto,

and oh yes, Isabel,
the longed-for fluttering

of my nap-time lids:
entrancing gold

of the first revealing dawns,
the first indispensable lullabies—

from

The Crossed-Out Swastika (2012)

ELEGY WITH AN OWL IN IT

The young, the war-buffeted, the banished—
they were blossom-and-fruit-seeking

branch lovers,
braid-in-the-inkwell schemers,

and their time under watchtowers,
brief as relinquished myrrh,

brisk as an owlet fluttering against
a soldier's insignia.

THE RAVINE

"The Holocaust by Bullets," Ukraine, 1941–1944,
Nina Raufimovna Lisitsina

In my fifth
holy year on earth,

undeterred,
I climbed out of a corpse-filled,

breaksprit ravine,
clutching the roots of trees

(so beautiful,
the god-tall cypresses,

the grandfather pines
in that part of the Crimea),

and groped my way, gingerly,
toward my twilit village,

the lone, itinerant survivor.
The pull, the rose light

of home
is unkillable.

THREE KINGS

When my belittled village was eclipsed
by pillaging soldiers,

quick as a windblown kite,
my baking aunt coaxed me

into her privy's acrid underworld.
Banished from the flour-dusted

blossoms of her apron,
I was too green to beseech God

or beautiful Queen Esther.
Unmoored, I fastened on the bookish

name of my slingshot,
Aramis, Aramis, Aramis—

as if in that shit-drenched dark,
I could summon, abracadabra,

its Y-shaped, trusty wood,
and from that musketeer mantra, I acquired

a little certainty, a little stamina, a little consolation,
like three resplendent kings

come to a filthy manger.

SALUTE

Dawn upon dawn,
my father's whereabouts

a fierce morsel in the mouth of a sphinx;
for sixty fogbound years,

not a word, and then
a key-cold message from Russia:

Father's remains
had been recovered and interred

in a resting place
for fallen Germans.

Month after abrading month,
my mother had mailed

a tin-kept sum to ensure
the burial of luckless

soldiers lost abroad,
then spurred me,

with her dying breath,
to solve the mystery—

Suffused with the titan birches' beauty,
dressed in overdue

atoms of grief—
my mother's persistent charity

miraculously repaid—
suddenly I witnessed,

past my father's terse marker,
two white unhampered horses

saunter from the haze-wrapped woods,
and halt—

their riffled manes
dazzling as epaulettes.

And after a bygone calm
that the breeze-swept stallions lowered

like an unbelievable drawbridge,
I clutched my shawl,

remembering Mother's elating,
live-and-let-live laugh,

as she claimed Father so favored
his saddle and ambling bay,

God must have given him
the soul of a centaur—

Then the pert allies
vanished into the haze,

the wind-tugged woods—
Dawn upon dawn,

and the hush after the kudos
of their trumpet-clear hooves:

Silence is the keenest salute.

JULIEK'S VIOLIN

Even here?
In this snowbound barracks?

Suddenly, the illicit sounds
of Beethoven's concerto

erupt from Juliek's smuggled violin,
suffusing this doomsday shed

teeming with the trampled
and the barely alive,

realm of frostbite and squalor,
clawing panic and suffocation—

Insane, God of Abraham,
insanely beautiful:

a boy insisting
winter cannot reign forever,

a boy conveying his brief,
barbed-wired life

with a psalmist's or a cantor's
arrow-sure ecstasy—

One prison-striped friend
endures to record

the spellbinding strings,
the woebegone,

and the other,
the impossible Polish fiddler,

is motionless by morning,
his renegade instrument

mangled
under the haggard weight

of winter-killed, unraveling men.
Music at the brink of the grave,

eloquent in the pitch dark,
tell-true, indelible,

as never before,
as never after—

Abundance,
emending beauty,

linger in the listening,
the truth-carrying soul of Elie,

soul become slalom-swift,
camp-shrewd, uncrushable;

abundance, be here, always here,
in this not-yet-shattered violin.

A GREAT BEAUTY

And when her son never returned
from the meant-to-crush-him camps,

the crucible of Poland,
always-hard-at-work Isa slept

for endless hours,
and once, under her lids, she was led,

by diligent female Virgils,
to a vast meadow

where an inspirited Isa embraced,
one by one,

countless women who remained
in mourning for their cherished sons.

Gallant and stricken,
together the myriad bereaved

but defiant women formed
an ever-widening circle,

prodigal with bitter tears,
and then, suddenly,

like a jackdaw darting
from eave to sun-drenched eave,

something flew between the throats
of the grieving,

heart-gutted mothers,
and a great beauty arose:

In the dream, Isa recalled,
the singing of the harrowed women

with war-taken sons
hushed the world's barrenness.

In the dream, the startling river of sound
altered the embattled earth.

AUSCHWITZ, ALL HALLOWS

Look, we have made
a counterpoint

of white chrysanthemums,
a dauntless path

of death-will-not-part-us petals
and revering light;

even here,
even here

before the once-wolfish ovens,
the desecrating wall

where you were shot,
the shrike-stern cells

where you were bruised
and emptied of your timebound beauty—

you of the confiscated shoes
and swift-shorn hair,

you, who left,
as sobering testament, the scuffed

luggage of utter hope
and harrowing deception.

Come back, teach us.
From these fearsome barracks

and inglorious fields
flecked with human ash,

in the russet-billowing hours
of All Hallows,

let the pianissimo
of your truest whispering

(vivid as the crunched frost
of a forced march)

become a slowly blossoming,
ever-voluble hearth—

revealing to us
(the baffled, the irresolute,

the war-torn, the living)
more of the fire

and attar of what it means
to be human.

from

More Than Peace and Cypresses (2004)

THE WAY OF *DUENDE*

Only mystery allows us to live,
only mystery.
—Lorca

I. NIGHT MIND

The day mind gone, Lord,
and all the stringencies,
the day's bright yokes, the day's heavy
bridles of status:
flamenco as an impassioned
celebration of night,
of *duende*, of mystery's
warrens and arabesques—
Romans, Carthaginians, phantom
Moors wander through the redemptive,
incantatory dancing—
a séance enticing
the ghosts of many taciturn
olives, almonds, bulls
and sun-beaten hills,
an *adios* to the unjust heat,
when the lack-land, roistering gypsies seem
the green moon's and the falling star's
rightfully appointed heirs;
in zealous summer,
the most prosperous among us all.

II. NAKED

To see your back, gypsy,
your shaved torso,
naked in the zealous
summer heat,
your eyes a goading,
a dark and sobersided blue I've found
only in Andalusia,
is to remember the rugged earth
swept clean of stallions,
reedless, futureless—
is to feel, Jacinto,
the tallow-pale quiet
of a runaway horse
at rest, the teeming,
swiftly marshaling silence
after the preening castanets—
taproot, crestfallen toad, hiding violet—
that same heart-lapping mystery,
that same stilling of the senses...

III. JACINTO INVOKING THE *DUENDE*

So Jacinto preens, cajoles, marshals
his expressive hips and boots
to sense *duende*
hidden in the darkest watermark,
the roguish wine stain
queering Juanillo's shirtfront—

What goblin wind, what glory
seizes him while he dances?—

Once, I swore, a piston-swift stag
had taken his place—

Tonight there is only the rakehell
laughter and torrential beauty,
the roar and daring
of unflappable *duende*
hard at work in the sudden
gusto of Jacinto,
as, in a flash,
Lorca's spirit is ensconced
at a corner table,
vibrant, vehement, applauding,
Lorca the presiding god—

Donde está Jacinto?
Vanished, absconded,
his eagle-eaten heart
whisked over Andalusian meadows, estuaries—

Seville, stand on tiptoe,
or the river of his *duende*
will drown you—

IV. THE WAY OF *DUENDE*

Not drowning, not burial,
not avalanche, no:
duende caresses you
with what seem, at first,
mandarin-soft hands,
until they strike you:
Now I will make you, make you, make you
god-drunk, cliff-defying—

Suddenly the piquant, the enigmatic,
the sheerly authentic
suffuses the stage,
the authentic, death's consort:

Jacinto's dance steps, agile
then aggrieved, inconsolable—

What is it that makes us gasp?
What is it that makes us wait,
stock-still?

Flame coursing through us,
flame—

Dust devil, shadow king,
figure in a fever dream...

From THE DEATH OF VINCENT VAN GOGH

I. THE MAELSTROM

The martial yellow of the field,
the sullying, ambushing wind and wheat:
foundered priest, indefensible apostle,
he knows each thing he sees
will become a heresy:
crows like brigands, brusque
Saracens in the canvas,
a green and russet road
through the vehement wheat.

In Auvers-sur-Oise, July's
belligerence, merciless July's
muzzling heat:
above the wheat rows, the open country,
the lantern-stern sun,
menacing, unjust, and God's
all-suffusing elegance,
the valley of Adam
not findable,
the shrewish pistol shrieks,
not here, not here:
one shot for the washaway scarecrow
carrot-maned, ugly, impolite, sick—
Red boots,
ceaseless, arduous—
The brigand crows take wing, take wing.
The mountebank crows take—

Coal-hot and auburn pauper,
he lumbers back to the village,
ransacked, unraveling:
red palms, red pittance—
the land, the downfall yellow, and the day
his maelstrom.

CATECHISM IN THE GARDEN OF FIVE PINES

Sh! The old women of Villalba del Alcor
are talking.
When brusque soldiers came,
tiny sisters, they hid
behind a stand of bearded irises
like chivalrous *señores.*

What is time to the women,
what is memory?

In their garden of five pines,
the years pass,
further and further away
from Franco.
The sibilant fountain,
the unremitting spring, has no sense
of civil war;
the cradling earth, the clear water
are no longer colored by chaos,
by the crimson of many Cains and Abels.

And where has the blood gone?
Is the blood ever stanched?
Not the blood
but the spirit of the blood
teems, still percolates
beneath Iberian ground,
still troubles the indomitable sisters,
the eyewitness galaxies of olives.

Why weren't the olives
a shield,
silver-green or a gauntlet

when stealthy fascists intrigued
to murder the poet?

Mute to the human,
they had no sway,
no dominion over
the undeterred pistols,
they could only lament to the persistent
altar candle of the summer moon:
Hands and arms for what?

Lord, Lord, my unflagging
blacksmith and maker,
for what unrivaled aim,
for what annealing reason
was I forged?

You have hands to minister
and receive manna;
you have arms to clasp
the larkish solace of children,
ears to absorb
the world's rumors,
to incorporate
the telltale, the human.

And if the news of the human brings me
only terror,
if the news of the human
is only havoc?
In the garden of five pines,
the years pass
but not the rumors, the harrowing
reports of the poet's end:
in a *barranco*, a bleak gully,
at the last,

a bullet in his backside
for loving men—
Is the world that broken-toothed,
that brutal?

The world is justice-starved, vast,
its kings incorrigible,
and fear is the aphrodisiac:
Beware! Beware! The poet cried.
This life is not a dream!

Poet, lodestar,
lover of men—
I am love! I am nature!—
is it only in genial dreams
that freedom lives?
Is it real
the road to paradise?

Like Isis in Andalusia,
you'll follow the roadside
I revered,
through the raven-dark field
where the moon roams,
un-persecuted, seeking
the little paradise of the Tamarit,
treasurable orchard
where I dreamed without end—
unerring, you'll embrace
the fecund plain
where I veered, blindfolded
but never effaced.

In the knockabout, warring world
what will I face?
A gag or a blindfold?
Will my freedom
be stripped from me?
In the garden of five pines now,
tell me,
what is the worst?
What is the worst
that can happen?

More terrible than the heart's carnage,
to walk the road to paradise
as if the road were leprous,
to journey, immutable,
a flat-worlder, a trudging sleepwalker
in realms of jasmine,
precincts of showy verbena,
wandering scornfully amid
pealing bells, ringing anvils,
voluptuous pageantry,
forever reticent or stony, forever
gutted or stuffed with straw:
at each anniversary,
in every season, an impassive
stranger on this earth.

MORE THAN PEACE AND CYPRESSES

More than peace and cypresses, emboldened
hares at the field's edge,

Father, I love
gallantry, tenacity, the sanguine

heart before the ledge:
the artist questing and failing —

the feet of bested Icarus
plunging into the sea's crest —

the artist triumphing: a page of fire
from the book of heroes.

More than light-hooved gazelles, views
from the mizzenmast,

enlivening shores,
more than soldier-still lilies, I love

the torchlike men who've taught me —
past the rueful

glitter of lucre and guns,
past the starkness of the lynching tree—

the truth-or-bust beauty
of passion transformed

into sheer compassion,
true shouldering,

and common as breath, common as breath,
the extravagant wheel of birth and death.

from

Beautiful Signor (1997)

From LOVE POEM OF THE ROMAN DAYS

II. THE VIEW FROM VIA SANNIO

Sunday: the market's still, the street,
gossipless and serene.
Above the basilica,
the Roman sky blooms,
as never before,
and I must wake you,
give you this view,
garnet, roseate, gill-blue—
A gull delights
in San Giovanni's facade,
the pale row of mystics,
passing from crown to crown—

We love the morning man,
saint of the neglected,
neighbor blessing the esplanade
with glinting scraps,
morsels for the gruff, masterless cats
ensconced by the ancient wall—
hands full, coat pockets
fecund with coins,
to affirm we are all
bishops and kings,
beggars and stewards—

For us, in our ardor,
there's only one sill,
one city.

From THE RISK-TAKERS

XI.

And I find in you
the ocher and gold,
the lustrous, silvery green
of the olive fields above Assisi.
And I find in you
the ineffable pink
of the renowned saint's
open palms,
the white, like fountain foam,
of an unabashed
almond in bloom,
find in you
the sky with a linnet blue
of our Brother Wind's scapular:

of this spectrumed love,
always remember
there is an allaying portion left
for the Sister Larks,
the beggar's makeshift bowl—

Sometimes this utmost praise
braves the world
barefoot, conversant with stones
and seraphim:
oh here is a caress,
an empathy to quell
the prowling wolf,
a calm of bundled arrows, doves...

From THE MAGICIAN-MADE TREE

VI. THE RIVER GOD

On a Sabbath walk, we learn both of our first loves
died in our youth.
We stray off the road;
in the simmering dusk,
in the coppice's wild quiet,
our discomfiting clothes
scattering—a little flurry
in the lizard kingdom—
your skin in a matchless
garment of shadow,
evocative of a statue
in a spare museum room:
Michelangelo's *Model of a River God.*

Like us, the Renaissance genius puzzled
why rustic deities and lovers
sally into love, arrayed
only in flesh, bruisable flesh,
if the tournament's end is always
willowy mourning:

against the undertow,
your body, siphoned for a while
of sorrow—
will I ever love you more
than in this place
where voices of reproach
can't reach us,
all the meshes of dismay—

your irrepressible cry
navigating the insurgent thighs
Buonarotti bends
to fashion out of clay.

THE HUMMINGBIRD

Bright whirligig that knows no grief,
sudden gem whose engine
is diligent and beatific,
in pure communion,
I've opened and taken you
deep into my being.

Scion to your quick colors,
your tiny hosannas, I poise
before my love's body
become a thousand thimbles of weeping
for dawn,
keen galaxy I'd test and savor
with a deft, regaling bill:
all this majesty is for me—

Now the hours are deities
of nectar and sweat.
Now the hours are flower-gorged,
filled with his breath—

Suddenly, I'm flying
backward,
fleet hovering in the moment,
breakneck marionette:
grit gone, God yes,
and panic's balcony:
the carnage in the eye burned away—

FROM THE THEATER OF WINE

Suddenly we're sons of Noah,
in biblical robes,
wielding showy censers
to start with pomp
a Rosh Hashanah preschool pageant.
When the whirling incense
clears from the open courtyard
of the old kabbala school,
and the small children have quelled
their raucous coughing,
barrels of ripeness are brought in,
and tin pans
brimming with the vineyards' glory.
Soon Noah's mightily confused,
mock intoxicated...

As you take a jesterly bow,
autumn sun glistens in the auburn
of your Old Testament wig.
And spry Noah is filling
the lush, tousled lap
of his lavish beard
with grapes.
And the barefoot children are learning
a fruit-breathed laughter,
as they stamp and savor the labor
in the jubilant lesson of wine.

BEAUTIFUL SIGNOR

All dreams of the soul
End in a beautiful man's or woman's body.
—Yeats, "The Phases of the Moon"

Whenever we wake,
still joined, enraptured—
at the window,
each clear night's finish
the black pulse of dominoes
dropping to land;

whenever we embrace,
haunted, upwelling,
I know
a reunion is taking place—

Hear me when I say
our love's not meant to be
an opiate;
helpmate,
you are the reachable mirror
that dares me to risk
the caravan back
to the apogee, the longed-for
arms of the Beloved—

Dusks of paperwhites,
dusks of jasmine,
intimate beyond belief

beautiful Signor

no dread of nakedness

beautiful Signor

my long ship,
my opulence,
my garland

beautiful Signor

extinguishing the beggar's tin,
the wind of longing

beautiful Signor

laving the ruined country,
the heart wedded to war

beautiful Signor

the kiln-blaze
in my body,
the turning heaven

beautiful Signor

you cover me with pollen

beautiful Signor

into your sweet mouth—

This is the taproot:
against all strictures,
desecrations,

I'll never renounce,
never relinquish
the first radiance, the first
moment you took my hand—

This is the endless wanderlust:
dervish,
yours is the April-upon-April love
that kept me spinning even beyond
your eventful arms
toward the unsurpassed:

the one vast claiming heart,
the glimmering,
the beautiful and revealed Signor.

from

Soul Make a Path Through Shouting (1994)

From DOWN FROM THE HOUSES OF MAGIC

I.

Now the moon darns the moor with its fabric of willows
And the sea rushes with the ecstasy of ants.
Down from the houses of magic, a healing wind sweeps,
Down from the houses of magic.
On Gull Hill, in the flaming garden, God flings
A fistful of robin redbreast—razzamatazz.
And the reed of the supple mind bends and shivers,
And the choirlike, match-stemmed, fiercely gallant flowers:
Johnny-jump-up, pert buttercup, anemone, peony, lupine,
The first lightning-white rose dying to open,
Beneath the systole and diastole of a starry night,
Bee-yellows, butter-yellows, sweet-simmering-hay-yellows,
Iris, allium, the proffered chalices of dark tulips
(The colors of a fabulous dusk in Tunisia).
Coming soon, a pleasure of freesias, a pleasure!
Tintinnabulation!
All the prayer-wheels of April-into-May luster
Spinning God-drunk—till finally beside
The moon-daft willow, slack as a marionette,
The yellow frenzy of scotch broom,
The fleet-souled orioles marshal, at wolf's hour,
Than sally in one brilliant will.

SOUL MAKE A PATH THROUGH SHOUTING

for Elizabeth Eckford

Thick at the schoolgate are the ones
Rage has twisted
Into minotaurs, harpies
Relentlessly swift;
So you must walk past the pincers,
The swaying horns,
Sister, sister,
Straight through the gusts
Of fear and fury,
Straight through;
Where are you going?

I'm just going to school.

Here we go to meet
The hydra-headed day,
Here we go to meet
The maelstrom—

Can my voice be an angel-on-the-spot,
An amen corner?
Can my voice take you there,
Gallant girl with a notebook,
Up, up from the shadows of gallows trees
To the other shore:
A globe bathed in light,
A chalkboard blooming with equations—

I have never seen the likes of you,
Pioneer in dark glasses:
You won't show the mob your eyes,

But I know your gaze,
Steady-on-the-North-Star, burning—

With their jerry-rigged faith,
Their spear of the American flag,
How could they dare to believe
You're someone sacred?:
Nigger, burr-headed girl,
Where are you going?

I'm just going to school.

SUNG FROM A HOSPICE

Still craving a robust
Tenderness and justice,
I will go on living
With all I have seen:
Young men lusterless;
Against my blind cheek—
Blessed be the frangible
And dying,
The irreplaceable dead—
In my crestfallen arms:
With breath,
Then without it,
With flesh,
Then freed of it—

And the indurate man I heard
Condemn the stricken,
While my cousin was dying,
If he had walked these wards,
Armorless, open
To the imperiled,
Surely he would have gleaned
To sit in judgment
Is to sit in hell—

Lesions, elegies,
Disconnected phones—

Rain, nimble rain,
Be anodyne,
Anoint me
When I say outright:
In the plague time, my heart
Was tested,

My living soul
Struck like a tower bell,
Once, twice,
Four times in a single season.

POEM FOR THE ARTISTS OF THE HOLOCAUST

The bone-white wind of this century
A prayer-shawl of human ash.
And still the hand lifts
The intrepid pencil,
The chip of charcoal,
Against the plunder, the ordure, the roaring.

And still the soul craves to make bridgeable
The space between the careworn
And the dead,
Craves never to quit the embattled earth
Unrecorded,
The unstainable soul:

This is the charnel house art,
The epistle,
Cached in the sleep-safe tin,
Inviolable, brought to air:

Dear Finder,

In Terezin,
By the meager bread-carts,
In Auschwitz,
Beside the rooms of shaved hair,
Tell someone I was here.

FLEUR

No, it is not suffering that engenders it
            it is beyond suffering,
The Flower—
            though it rests beside
the tears, the million barricades,
            fusillade upon fusillade...
it rests,
            soft as a fontanel.

*

Fifty-four whales beach on the shore,
            vials of blood, and syringes,
so that we might perceive The Flower,
            cry out for it.

*

With sternness and delicacy,
            Georgia O'Keeffe,
that clear-eyed woman,
            leaned into its sacred warmth,
with her paints,
            her probity.

*

Yes, its stem is like
            the jammed, astonishing column of crutches
the healed leave behind,
            a column of miracles
in a snow-lit, hallowed shrine.

*

Stopping on the road to Tula,
to Tolstoy's estate,
I found a flower
like one from my childhood,
a great seraphic bloom.
But there were missiles between it
and its Western twin,
missiles!, missiles!,
and a killing mystique.

*

Not long after Chernobyl's gasp,
I looked from a window
in Dostoyevsky's house,
and watched a man pass a sinister wand
over the vegetables for market,
over the flowers.

*

How much can the petals withstand,
while we hasten the leavings,
the radioactive waste?

*

It cannot last,
this juggernaut, this whirlwind futility:
surely joy will outdistance
the century's mass graves,
the earth's furious junkyards;
surely joy will outdistances us.

*

A woman strokes the numerals
seared forever into her skin,

and with deadsure fingers examines
stark photographs from the war:
this happened to me,
and this—
and still I survived…
Yes, there were lupines in the camp,
and our joy in them was real,
as real as our misery.
We would find some little corner of the barracks
to put them on display;
we would pick and scoop them into our arms,
after a day of forced labor.

*

Oh once, during the war,
there was a boy,
bewildered, deaf from birth,
unable to comprehend
the men in dark uniforms barking
Jew, Jew,
get down on your knees!—
so that his father had to coax him
to touch the paving with his mouth,
to take part in the wretched street cleaning,
And after wetting a stone
with a sullen tongue,
the boy found his work
had made it shine.

Then ridicule, and bullying hatred,
then indignity gave way
to something rapt—gave way
to sheer accomplishment.

Undaunted, he found a tiny flower-shape
set deep into the stone,

let its brief, invisible pollen brush him.

And for that one instant, let me believe,
the universe was moved;
all the gall of the day
was changed to wine:

ma fleur, ma fleur...

Oh what would you give to find that flower?

from

The Mud Actor (1982)

THE CHILD YOU CALL EEYORE

for Kenzaburo Oe and his fictional fathers

Your son tosses, sweet idiot wrapped
in sleep, in sweat.
You stand above him, the father, rumpled and phantom,
at zenith: In the dark he opens
his weak eyes, lifts
his small sleeves of fat. A shrill sob
shakes the room.
And you hold him, envelop him: the child
you call Eeyore, your brain-damaged child, your holocaust
of a firstborn.

What you live with: At first
you wanted him to die; you tried to flee, then chose
forbearance. Now, together, you form
a planet. You notice everything: his fear
of the toothbrush, his love of motion, how his face lights
on the subway train—
the bond, the conduit between you
so supernatural, that when Eeyore burns
his hand on the stove, far away, in your office,
you feel the singe and cry
yourself: a man whose heart and senses
become a womb—

In wintry Tokyo, I find you,
two Eskimos, a fat
father and son,
trudging home at dusk from a full day
on the trains.

You say you would go down into the grave
with your child, as you brush thin snow
from his brow.

It is a tenderness beyond witness.

THE MEMORY OF HIROSHIMA

for the survivors and for myself

The people of Hiroshima ask nothing of the world except that we be allowed to offer ourselves as an exhibit for peace.

-Shinzo Hamai, Mayor of Hiroshima, 1949

We believed we would be safe in Hiroshima.
We boarded the train
with our burden of rice cakes
and rolled mats, toys, swaddling clothes,
and cardboard luggage
tied with a string.
We were a family
of four children, fleeing
starvation, the endless lists
of the war dead,
forced to leave behind
our widowed mother
and ailing grandmother;
we were entrusted with an uncle
who lived secure
in Hiroshima.
It was the hope
of hegira—
three days of hard travel
to a kinder life—
the wing words
of a Nō play:
"We go, our hearts unhindered
as the flight of clouds..."
In time, there was only

the slow ribbon of our journey
unwinding under the sky,
the dull rocking of the cars,
the windows scrolls of green,
as the trains steamed
through planets of rice, the land
dotted with pillboxes.
Always I sat in stiff seats, facing
my older sister, Michiko,
cached in her dark, proper traveling dress,
so wrong for Japanese summer,
the baby, Taiji, lively in her arms,
her thin, inquisitive brows
the black winged traces
of my sumi brush
—while Isamu, in his schoolboy's cap,
drummed his knees to a fine tattoo,
or tapped the window.
To calm him,
I took from a box
the gold-braided German marionette
my grandfather gave me
as a boy,
and recited strands
of a puppet play
—a beautiful *michiyuki* passage.
In the moment of performance,
working the strings,
I felt the warm, ingenuous gaze
of an old couple,
two passengers across the aisle,
and craved
invisibility, the black anonymous clothes
of a puppeteer's apprentice,
that could free me to be,
not Yoshi Nakamura,
but the shadow of a doll,

masterful and hidden
from death,
hidden, at seventeen,
from the carmine paper
of a draft notice,
from the terrible pledge:
Yes, I would die,
I would die for the emperor.
I closed my eyes and recovered,
in one long breath,
Doolittle's raid:
the panic of parasols,
the crush of running bodies
against the lunch stand,
bowls of seaweed soup splattering
on the counter,
as my brother, Mamoru, was knocked
from the wooden stool—
my last glimpse of him
a ripped sleeve, a small window
filled with flesh,
that simply vanished.
I opened my eyes,
put the puppet away, remembering
our fruitless search
as an earlier maze
of Tokyo streets meshed
with a world of aisles and strange depots,
as a needle of trains threaded a weariness
from station to station:
Isamu vomiting on the platform,
the sting of the baby's cry;
the haggard mask of my face
in the glass,
stars, leaves, clear landscapes
flowing through it,
and the image of my mother

in shadow, at the family shrine,
wiping the photographs of the dead—

On the last night,
there was a note of moonlight
pinned to our seats,
its white message finally
passing over our faces—
the moon itself,
a dropped camellia,
a strange and distant bloom,
as I watched
my sister's sleeping form, noting
the black thick-heeled shoes
that hurt her so,
and in her moonlit lap,
the rhododendron flower
picked near Kyoto.

After the black music of ruined cities,
Tokyo, Osaka, Kobe,
we found Hiroshima at dawn,
on the morning of the fourth,
beautiful, intact,
the river Tenma tinged
with gold and pomegranate.
We walked from Yokogawa station
till the sky paled,
following the meanders of the river
to the house
near Sumiyoshi bridge,
where we found the poignant eyes
of Noburu,
who did his best to hide
his bad limp
under his *yukata*.
To our surprise,
he had another guest

as well, a young postal clerk,
Shinkichi, who added to
the noisy and jubilant reunion:
tears of saké
dribbling onto a sleeve,
the skin around our eyes deepened
to a plum blush.

On the second day,
Michiko stepped out for fish,
the blue fabric of the morning—pierced
by a siren.
At the all-clear, we men roused
for tea and talk,
the gentle swaying of the fans
over the low table.
There was a lacquered screen
beside me, the carved arc
of a maple:
In Japan, always
the delicate, deciduous branch,
the gentle sadness
of autumn in the soul,
even in summer.
The panel was open; I could see
a stone lantern,
a swatch of shade tree.
In the kitchen, on a cutting block,
were the shards
of a blue teacup, splinters
of vermilion reeds:
my morning clumsiness,
my habit of pressing the warm teacup
to my cheek,
whenever I was lost
in thought.
I had just wiped

the stained hem of my *yukata.*
Isamu was playing in the yard.
The baby was asleep
in the next room.
We were talking about
work, the politics of the war,
when I veered away,
imagining out loud
a lazy escape
under the shade tree.
The impact came
at the moment of soft laughter.
There was a shock of light.
The house shredded.
The impression of the day,
which was the hushed wedding
of white and gold,
of summer light brushed
on paper panels,
became black and crushed.
I did not know
what to do:
I no longer seemed to have
a body,
only a feeling of searching
through cruel heat and ash.
In my mind's eye, I tried to lift
the baby, Taiji,
and then, suddenly, I realized
we were dead.
I hovered near the wreckage,
in shock.
It looked as if
someone had taken
the silver flat of an iron
and pressed it into the city.
Then, gradually,
I felt myself rising toward

a great and welcoming light.

*

Now, coming out of a mountain tunnel,
I shield my eyes from the sudden explosion
of sunlight, catching
the brief rumor of my face
in the glass,
and know that I am Cyrus Cassells,
riding on a train
to Hiroshima,
clasping a memory
no one can explain away,
rippling back and forth
between worlds,
as if all time
were the surface of a single pond,
as if the soul
were a radio, and each station
were a life, an incarnation,
which could be yielded
by the turning of a mental dial,
the mind of a young traveler
turned to give you
Yoshi Nakamura
in World War II Japan.
I think of death and beyond,
how I learned
that Mamoru did not die
but was sheltered
by a candy-maker and his wife,
then enticed to live
as their adopted son
—a wartime tale
of enchantment,
how I saw our mother Omie

alone, dispossessed, taken in at last
by her in-laws,
only to die one winter
shortly after the war.
And what is one family's death
on the killing floor of history?
Not the panoply of war,
the terms of conflict,
what the soul remembers
is love:
a search through the snow
of ash and ruined flesh
for my lost Michiko, Isamu, Taiji,
a search through a thousand Tokyo streets
for Mamoru—
I look from the train
—towns, fields gliding by me
on my pilgrimage,
and feel
a perfection, an order, a brotherhood so literal
it dazes me, for truly
we are each other,
and if our legacy
is obscenity, ceaseless war,
and war, a fathomless falling away
from consciousness,
then this is the nightmare
we all wake from;
let us wake out of the nightmare—annealed.
We who have the duty to refuse
to kill, we who have the genius, the power,
to darn our world,
we who are both human and divine,
if we could stand together at last, in the place
where the victim and murderer embrace,
where there is no enemy, no evil,
no guilt nor judgment,
only ourselves

and this juggernaut of fear,
if we could stand,
and you could take from me
the memory of Hiroshima,
as a bit of burden
to cup in your hands, a share of ash
to scatter in gentle wind
as a talisman against all war,
for whoever holds the memory of Hiroshima
there is no choice
but peace.

I believe I died
to know the lust for peace,
to know fully and forever
the sacredness of life cannot be sacrificed
for any end.
And I want to tell you
how in the museum
I had to stop myself from crying out
at the photographs of Hiroshima
that matched my lucid dreams and recall,
how I looked at the singed
and terribly wounded *hibakusha*
without recoil, swabbing them with my eyes, my love,
because I recognized and claimed at last
my own experience—
these are my people
also, this is what we chose
for ourselves, for you,
and for the world to remember,
as unconsciously we chose to die
in protest, trying to say
the quality of life is more important
than survival—
how I learned that the soul can cradle
so much suffering, so much horror
and still remain whole.

Last night, in the youth hostel, I dreamed again
the hell screen of the bombing.
A blinding flash.
A brutal shattering of the panes.
Again, women and children dressed in flames,
a human smoke.
Everywhere the charred weeping of blood,
the damaged wrappers of skin.
The country of ash. The country of ash.
Today, in the August sun, I walk,
one week after the anniversary,
with my friends, Atsushi and Takayoshi,
always seeing against the sky
the raw, obstinate, cracked-shell statement
of the Atomic Dome.
And what can I say,
in the Hiroshima jazz club,
to the young Japanese, who,
searching my eyes for American guilt,
asks me, "Cyrus, do you feel shame in Hiroshima?":
"No, can you understand,
I believe I died *here?"*—

I had to retrace my steps;
I had to make myself walk
through the sound of my own
weeping for the world,
to crawl again, from memory,
across the charred keening floor
of Hiroshima,
the thick dream I move through
like a mud actor,
a blight of rooftiles, splintered wood,
fumes and searing heat,
through the ragged breathing and the netted sounds
of the dying,

which are indistinguishable
from those of the newborn,
to crawl through the bald epiphany of the words
I am still alive,
beyond the useless tatters
of my own flesh,
and the map of trauma
—which has vanished now,
amid river sounds, a noisy relief
of children.
I had to return, once again,
as a visitor,
because I believe
not one consciousness was destroyed
in Hiroshima.
I had to hear
the purposeful ring of the peace bell,
to see the bronze figure
of Sadako Sakichi,
with her arms uplifted and gently weighted
with the many paper cranes
that are Japanese blessings.
I had to find and embrace
the deep form and unity of the world.
It is the new flesh, the sun's cleansing, the crane's flight,
flecked with remembered ash.
It is the heartbeat
of a reconstructed city, a slow walk
through Hiroshima, the sound of a radio
turning on. Everything in life
is resurrection.

—Hiroshima to San Francisco,
1978-1981

ACKNOWLEDGEMENTS

Many thanks to: my dynamic past and current editors and publishers (Copper Canyon Press, Four Way Books, Holt, Nine Mile Press, Southern Illinois University Press, and TCU Press); the late Al Young for taking a chance on a 23-year-old poet; Judy Karasik for being a fantastic and risk-taking first editor at Holt; Carolyn Forché for kindly inviting me to be both her personal assistant and later her colleague at George Mason; my mentors, Linda Gregerson, Stratis Haviaris, Galway Kinnell, Stanley Kunitz, William Merwin, Alan Shapiro, Timothy Steele, and Jean Valentine; to Cornelius Eady, Toi Derricotte, and the ever-expanding Cave Canem community of writers; to my peers who have buoyed me over the years: Sara Arvio, Margo Berdeshevsky, Olga Broumas, Victoria Chang, Mark Doty, Alison Deming, Rita Dove, Martín Espada, Suzanne Gardinier, Veronica Golos, Jorie Graham, Jessica Hagedorn, Joy Harjo, Ellen Hinsey, Marie Howe, the late Denis Johnson, Patricia Spears Jones, John Keene, Michael Klein, Li-Young Lee, Jane Miller, David Mura, Marilyn Nelson, Naomi Nye, Carl Phillips, Jayne Anne Phillips, Nicholas Samaras, Aaron Shurin, Patricia Smith, Susan Tichy, Cecilia Woloch, Mark Wunderlich, and Dominic Zuccone; to Rae Armantrout, Lorna Dee Cervantes, the late great Lucille Clifton, Camille Dungy, Ilya Kaminsky, Sandra Lim, Sharon Olds, Alicia Ostriker, David St. John, Evie Shockley, and Brian Turner for their active goodwill and support. A special thanks to Patrick Dougher for gracing this retrospective of my work with his deeply moving art.

ABOUT THE AUTHOR

Cyrus Cassells was born in Dover, Delaware, in 1957. He grew up in the Mojave Desert north of Los Angeles. He began writing poetry in high school. Cassells studied acting and received a B.A. from Stanford University in Film and Broadcasting in 1979.

Cassells is the author of *Is There Room for Another Horse on Your Horse Ranch?* (Four Way Books, 2024), a finalist for the National Poetry Series; *The World That the Shooter Left Us* (Four Way Books, 2022), a Housatonic Book Award finalist; *More Than Watchmen at Daybreak* (Nine Mile Books, 2020); *The Gospel According to Wild Indigo* (Southern Illinois University Press, 2018), a finalist for the NAACP Image Award, the Balcones Prize, and the Helen C. Smith Memorial Award from the Texas Institute of Letters; *The Crossed-Out Swastika* (Copper Canyon Press, 2012), a finalist for the Balcones Prize; *More Than Peace and Cypresses* (Copper Canyon Press, 2004), named a *Library Journal* Best Book of the Year; *Beautiful Signor* (Copper Canyon Press, 1997), winner of a Lambda Literary Award and a Sister Circle Book Award, a finalist for the Bay Area Book Reviewers Award, and nominated for the Pulitzer Prize; *Soul Make a Path Through Shouting* (Copper Canyon Press, 1994), named a *Publisher's Weekly* Best Book of the Year and nominated for the Pulitzer Prize, received the William Carlos Williams Award and was a finalist for the Lenore Marshall Prize and the AWP Book Prize Award; and *The Mud Actor* (Henry Holt & Co., 1982), a National Poetry Series selection and finalist for a Bay Area Book Reviewers Award.

Cassells is the recipient of a Pushcart Prize, the Peter I. B. Lavan Younger Poets Award, and fellowships from the Civitella-Ranieri Foundation, the Fine Arts Work Center in Provincetown, the Lannan Foundation, the Rockefeller Foundation, and the National Endowment for the Arts. *Still Life with Children: Selected Poems of Francesc Parcerisas* (Stephen F. Austin State University Press, 2019), and *To The Cypress Again and Again: Tribute to Salvador Espriu* (Stephen F. Austin State University Press, 2023), translated from the Catalan, were both awarded the Texas Institute of Letters biennial Soeurette Diehl Fraser Award for Best Translated Book. In 2019, Cassells was nominated for a Pulitzer Prize in Criticism for his film and television reviews in *The Washington Spectator.*

Cassells has worked as a translator, film critic, actor, and teacher. A 2019 Guggenheim Fellow, Cassells lives in Austin and teaches at Texas State University, where he is currently a Regents' Professor and a University Distinguished Professor of English. In 2021, he received a Texas State University Presidential Award for Scholarly/Creative Activities and was appointed Poet Laureate of Texas. In 2022, Cassells received an Academy of American Poets Laureate Fellowship to administer his statewide "What Juneteenth Means to Me" poetry contest for students in grades 8-12. He has recently served as the Guest Poetry Editor for the Academy of American Poets Poem-a-Day (National Poetry Month, April 2024) and curated a special issue on contemporary African American poets for the *New American Studies Journal* for the University of Göttingen in Germany.

ABOUT ELLEN HINSEY

Yale Younger Poet Ellen Hinsey is the author of nine books of poetry, essays, dialogue, and literary translation. A former Berlin Prize fellow of the American Academy in Berlin, she taught for many years at Skidmore College in Paris and has recently been a visiting professor at the University of Göttingen in Germany.